TACTILE
VALUES

New Issues Poetry & Prose

Editor	Herbert Scott
Associate Editor	David Dodd Lee
Advisory Editors	Nancy Eimers, Mark Halliday William Olsen, J. Allyn Rosser
Assistant to the Editor	Rebecca Beech
Assistant Editors	Lydia Melvin, Amy McInnis, Adela Najarro
Editorial Assistants	Karyn Kerr, Bethany Salgat
Business Manager	Michele McLaughlin
Fiscal Officer	Marilyn Rowe

Special thanks to: Scott Bade, Allegra Blake, Meggan Carney, Gabrielle Halko, Matthew Hollrah, Nancy Hall James, Alexander Long, Marianne Swierenga, and Bonnie Wozniak.

New Issues Poetry & Prose
The College of Arts and Sciences
Western Michigan University
Kalamazoo, Michigan 49008

First Edition, 2000.

ISBN: 0-932826-91-1 (paperbound)

Library of Congress Cataloging-in-Publication Data:
Scott, Mark
Tactile Values/Mark Scott
Library of Congress Catalog Card Number (99-76769)

Art Direction:	Tricia Hennessy
Design:	Valerie Fredenburgh
Production:	Paul Sizer
	The Design Center, Department of Art
	College of Fine Arts
	Western Michigan University
Printing:	Courier Corporation

TACTILE VALUES

MARK SCOTT

New Issues

WESTERN MICHIGAN UNIVERSITY

for Uncle Chuck, and for Loretta
the wished-for words . . .

Contents

I

Every Drift	9
Passive	10
Inner Life	11
Before Titles	13

II

First Death	21
After Practice	22
Drosophila	23
True Colors	24
Laps	25
Crush	26
Smartweed	27
The China Syndrome	28
Field Test	29
Tendrils	30
On a Bus in Torino	32
Initiation by Aphasia	34

III

Touch	39
The New Century	40
Freudian Tenderness	42
The Difference	44
The Tactile Dome	45
Concord Palinode	47
Lips	49

Architects 51

Branches 52

Blood Test 54

IV

The Last Twenty Pages 59

The Midnight Oil, an Ode to Psyche 60

Cherry, Birch, Ash 62

First Day of Spring 64

Thompson Creek Road 67

Dilation 68

Dawn Finished 69

A Friend 70

The Scott Boys 72

The Cave of AIDS 73

Accumulations 75

Fruit Country 77

When I Die 78

Viewers Like You 80

Acknowledgements

Earth Against Heaven: A Tiananmen Square Anthology:
   "The China Syndrome" Five Islands Press, Australia.

Fourteen Hills: "Fruit Country"

The Kenyon Review: "Every Drift"

Life on the Line: Selections on Words & Healing: "When I Die"
   Negative Capability Press.

The Paris Review: "Touch," "The Scott Boys,"
   "Freudian Tenderness," "The New Century"

Poetry: "The Cave of AIDS"

Raritan: "Accumulations," "The China Syndrome,"
   "A Friend," "First Day of Spring"

Seneca Review: "Thompson Creek Road"

Sites: "Architects," "Viewers Like You"

Western Humanities Review: "Drosophila," "Crush,"
   "Concord Palinode," "Before Titles"

. . . . I must have the illusion of being able to touch a figure,
I must have the illusion of varying muscular sensations inside
my palm and fingers corresponding to the various projections
of this figure, before I shall take it as real, and let it affect
me lastingly.

—*Bernard Berenson*, The Florentine Painters, *1896*

I

Speech of touch towards others should be sparingly used;
for discourse ought to be as a field, without coming home
to any man.

—Francis Bacon, "Of Discourse," 1612

Every Drift

"Bad" in these matters is never the right word,
    is it?
Here I can speak freely and at a smoother
    clip,
clipping the least from my former position
to preserve every drift
    and drift.

Proleptic, thrown back, thrown out—
    lurched—
I felt ahead more than saw, thought
    ahead,
if these can be called feelings,
didn't you? It looked as though
    you did.

Things put abroad like a tablecloth in check:
    castings
and tailings, strippings and failings,
    fallings-off.
What's more rapid than passage?
It was a pretty night: the tree
    was lit,

skaters took the ice, pretzels smoked,
    cars stopped
at green lights. But we were elsewhere—
    Bermuda,
I think it was—or you were, and our moods
trafficked in their separate regions
    onward.

Passive

for Amy

Passive to that I could have been
the long night through,
patient in the front seat there,
done anything for, open to.

The whole of our knowing was with your
sideways moving quite new,
kisses less shy, much moister:
you said, "I know you."

There had been lightning at dinner,
then rain you wanted nearer
with its mint of silver change
along the avenue, porches of the town.

Passion quick as yours
burst upon us awkwardly,
free at midnight from our longing:
fifteen years for me, five for you.

I said, "I've never been this close to you."
And now I cover my mouth with my hand
to keep the warm love in,
the wild-for, the always-have-been.

Inner Life

It was a little bit a disaster,
said a friend, so he left the country.
Italy was *much better, less stupid*
than New York City, he said, where,
according to the author he'd interviewed,
you don't see anybody without an appointment.

People are irritating, just a sentence
or a phrase, you know. Well, Stefano
is a nice person I think, but no,
I try not to listen to him at all.
He writes bad poetry and I don't care.
Well, maybe a few things. He showed me
some things this morning that weren't bad.

Nobody American lacked an inner life—
or seemed to—something he had lacked
for as long as he could remember.
He thought there might have been
a flicker once, when he fell in love
with a Japanese woman, but it was nothing.

I have no interior life, but that is not
the point. The point is that you try
to do something with language.
I want to write without persons.
I want to get this balcony scene
without mentioning the persons at all.

So he left Rome, years ago. Back here,
in the uncertainty of everything,
he feels ready *to be on the move,*

but sits still instead and reads
(though he never can sit still and read),
and listens to the rest of us complain.

I just like to read books and write.
That's it. But I am trying to finish
this thesis, and I have this novel
that I don't like much, but it's all right.
But the point is not the story. What is story?

Before Titles

"And so the old gardener blew his nose on a red pocket
    handkerchief . . ."
I had to consult Graves for that beginning,
it's so formal, but the rest is from memory.

Have a man come through the door with a gun in his hand;
the third man through the door gets killed;
—it's men, mostly, which is unfortunate,
but women should know.

A stranger comes to town,
someone takes to the road;
you come home, you leave home,
you come of age, you save the tiger.

"All movies are westerns," said Peckinpah.
"You put the hare in front of the hounds
and let the hounds chase the hare.
What I want to do is make a movie about

the third man through the door.
In the big shootout,"—I skip here—
"there are always three men who come through the door.
The first man is the hero, his name's above the title,

he wears white, his gun is drawn, and he's firing . . ."
I watched one that didn't fit this description,
but fit this: "Overblown adventure saga about search
for lost canyon of gold, with doublecrosses, conflicts,
    mysterious clues, etc. . . ."

". . . The second man might be looking the other way,
but he's either a youngster on the way up
or an oldster who's got respect. His hand is on the holster,
he's looking forward, he might get a ding on the arm. . ."

"Once I let a guy blow me";
"Blow me";
"He blew him away" (men again).

He misplaces a kiss (Chaucer);
She turns her back on him (divorce);
I wonder what happened to Libby Boucher
(where are the snows?—that one).

A movement of the soul,
a movement of the bowels:
you see the difference between an action and an episode;

"yet Virgil, writing of Aeneas, hath pretermitted
many things. He neither tells how he was born,
how brought up, how he fought with Achilles,
how he was snatched out of the battle by Venus;
but that one thing, how he came into Italy,
he prosecutes in twelve books";

"how he came into Italy":
but what was Italy before Aeneas came?
who cared about Aeneas then?—
these questions are irrelevant.

You tree a man, throw rocks at him,
get him down from the tree:
that's the Western, in a nutshell.

Oh, I could tell you stories:
the potential and the actual and the gulf between them fixed;
"that story," as Anne Sexton put it;

or truncation itself: "only the good die young";
the success story, the happy ending, the failure
" . . . made worse by pre-release tampering
that cut extremely long film, leaving
abrupt denouement, several loose ends."

More famously: the enginer hoist with his own petar.
We call that "reflexive form" these days.
Then there's drama, what's "dramatic":
it's always being on the side of the last speaker
(especially when he or she—Sophocles,
Shakespeare, Dorothy Parker—boils over
and says some good things).

We used to know these things:
how buildings got built,
how marriages were arranged;
but we never knew why people laughed,
or what made something funny,

or why people kept turning the page,
or why Impressionists and dogs kept selling,
or what it was about children and dogs
that so upstaged W.C. Fields;
even the difference between knowledge and belief
we called into question;

the difference, again, between
subject and theme, argument and thesis;
why there's more than one word for one thing

when "Nothing," as Woolf wrote, "is ever one thing";
how many things a book can be about
and still be about one big thing—

and somewhere here in my notes,
the key to all mythologies:
that, in a love affair, one doesn't take notes.

The key itself: the gates of ivory and horn,
if I remember correctly, sleep and sacrifice,
the Cave of Mammon—filthy lucre and all that shit.

"She thought she had to go to the bathroom,
but she was having a baby. She threw it out the window
and went back to bed."

It's in the distinction Forster made
between story and plot,
the one being, "This happened, and then that";
the other, "She died, and then he died of grief"

—as in King's "Exequy," to be with her:
"Stay for me there: I will not fail
To meet thee in that hollow vale.
And think not much of my delay:
I am already on the way."

That lie; otherwise, no love stories,
only tales of woe, gnashing of teeth—
as in the Old Testament, tit for tat,
quid pro quo, the terminal feud

that never ends, the house of Atreus;
or, in a Polybian mood,
the melodrama of republicanism:
Emerson meets Albee: you sit on a park bench
to think, and someone, a fellow citizen, asks,
"Do you have a headache?"

Assuming, of course, the whole "to think,"
the whole "a fellow citizen,"
when he or she may well be
just another consumer out to lunch.

"Super cast saddled with ludicrous script"—
not a great narrative, maybe, but serviceable.
Or Paul Taylor, from a sentence in Spinoza,
writing on the bodies of his dancers
a passage through the cloven kingdom:
"so fare our sever'd hearts."

Or not so fair. But I digress. Back at the ranch,
"The third man through isn't even a featured player;
he's coming in backwards and he's not sure
he's in the right movie. He gets to die before titles."

II

Tangere enim et tangi nisi corpus nulla potest res.
Lucretius, *De rerum natura*, I, 304

First Death

When I was almost ten,
my youngest brother
asked me to ride bikes with him.
I went to a movie with a friend.

I cried, that day,
because everyone else was crying.

Twenty years later,
I couldn't make the smallest decisions.
When asked in an office if I knew why,
I cried beyond my hour.

I should have gone with my brother on the bike.
I never saw him again.
I can't remember what he looks like.

After Practice

The other suits were blue or team-colored,
that Hawaiian print we had one summer,
but you wore white, and you were the tallest.
Your younger sister had the biggest shoulders,
did the best butterfly. Your youngest
owned the individual medley, all the strokes.
You were the best backstroker on the team.

It fascinated me that you were so tall, so thin.
I was younger, shorter, and did my swimming
stomach to the water, the three short-distance frees.
I'd watch you in the lanes, behind you in the water,
hand you my hand out of the pool on the deck,
then chase you up the stairs to the ice machine.

Once, I crawled under the clubhouse
across the cool stones to the window
of the locker room. I found it open,
clearing the hot shower's steam.
Your suit lay on the bench like a junked gardenia.
Your chest faced the wall of lockers,
your hands moved a towel on your shoulders,
between your breasts, down your lap.

I saw the whole back of you at ease relax.
Your white small looked small enough
to put my arms around, support with a hand.
Then you turned to look at what you felt
was looking in. I got back on my haunches
without the gravel sounding off, breathed
as if I'd swallowed water near the end of a race
but couldn't stop stroking, then leaned back in:
your brown arm made a brushing motion.

Drosophila

Dew-lover, we studied the laws
of the elementary game with you.
We set you up in a culture
you could multiply and be fruitful in,
a tapioca smooth as cream of wheat.
You gave it a malt of oxygen and waste,
like butter and brown sugar.
You twitched, indiscriminately,
and out of your pantagruel
we graphed heredity.

To keep from a failing grade—
I was more vinegar than you knew—
I cheated with your pepsin broth
that made my mouth secrete and quiver.
I stole the notes of lab partners
not even mine, grafting for myself
a better breed of result.

Smells crossed me with themselves:
the mimeo's fresh purple,
the salt off my partner's hands,
the gardenia oil on Julie's skin,
her jean-jacket's warm patchouli.

That was my yeast: you were the bad math
I did, the evidence I tampered with.
I probed too often with the prick,
dashed your reckless dishes with acid.
I crushed your population on a slide
that rode on your fluids, drosoplaning
between these two fingers that type
an accidental life of painful combinations.

True Colors

Did I steal a march on you
in some inhuman shape,
horse, chameleon, snake?
You thought I stalked you.
You called the campus police.
You called yourself a bitch,
later, and said it was a mistake.

All we did was take a walk.
The trouble was our talk,
the things we couldn't say.
Mine came later, on your floor,
in the poem of my salad days
I slipped under your door.

You were a dish; I was a tray:
longings firked up in us,
our roommates were in the way.
The walk we took was harmless—
until you took it wrong.
But I profaned it, too, I think.
I wanted to show you my true colors,
penny-brown and finger-pink.

Laps

The laps of women when I was young
have stood up. They were soft and warm,
and I would try to sleep in them.
Innocence was not in my head
when I was little in the laps of women,
when I was a kid now standing up.

Scars on her chin and top lip loved me
when I peeked up the body of Diana.
Becky was darker and had dimples.
I chose her shoulder at the hollow
made for the head, and pushed.

Brick was the lounge of Sara
when I moved and set my cheek
against her breasts, held my hands
between my thighs, bent up,
closed my eyes that see her now
stand up, and slept.

Sally had a dead top tooth
and a younger brother.
Her hair curled where it parted,
and in her arms I fell to dreams
as up the stairs she carried me.
When tucked in, down the laps of women I go.

Teenaged and stoned,
it was the car on the road
that rocked me to sleep
and slumped me over
Nancy's lap in the back seat.
Now all that is there and I am not.
Now the laps of women rise and go.

Crush

"To have a crush on someone"—
that's a schoolgirl's phrase,
the lexicographers say.

But I have a generalist's temperament
(like Napoleon's)
any aunt or schoolgirl can daunt and tether,

and I have had crushes all my life,
once on my aunt, my uncle's wife,
sometimes for many days together.

Crush,
ecrasez,
crescit sub pondere virtu:

What's so passing about it?
It's Byron's "Everything by turns
and nothing long,"

and you would have to have
Frank O'Hara's mental life
in Georg Simmel's metropolis

not to be ground up in its mills.
How pervious and flappable
can you afford to be?

"Marble does not laugh," said Diderot—
yes, but even marble twitches
intermittently.

Smartweed

In urns like Greeks my mother grows
geraniums and always has. The grapes
were crude cement frieze,
but the geraniums were lipstick
and singular in scent.
Not erect, brawling, grooved,
as weeds are described,
but spriggish, stemming, inflated.
To touch one was to know it
as petals fallen, aroma rising.
Each petal took a thumbnail
as a banana bruises, skin
keeping every score.
I liked to pass and nail a petal
for the pungency.

For the leaves, though:
they had cilia like my mother's cheeks,
rhythmic motion at a touch.
Their margin was crenate,
like that of the disks
that fluff the fields for the seeds.
There's a weed with this same
margin of geranium and disk.
They call it smartweed, I was told,
because it will grow anywhere.
In the back of a pickup,
in an inkling of soil mostly sand,
up against the cab, out of the wind—
six or seven smartweeds.

All they needed were urns and lipstick.
They had a home, and in me a mother.

The China Syndrome

Everything—gravel, books, and weeds—
has roots in China, goes there
to disappear. Where explanation ends,
China begins to revolve in the ear.
Like a shovel-full of dirt or stones
thrown to a destination, China's
loosely holding together whatever
aggregates, coheres, seems to want to
keep its shape. Our front driveway's
three-quarter inch river-washed gravel,
where it is that still; where it isn't,
where did it go? I asked my father,
he said China. And the other day I heard
not one but three mothers say,
that that's where the roots of bindweed go.
Our gardens and our driveways
turn up like loons, but where you'd
expect them to, as the rule of the saying
conducts them, as it yields.
Shame on us, though, if we say
China's reaping what we have sown—
holes without bottom lines,
weeds with absurd longevity,
gravel whose heaviness runs deep.
The books tell another story:
here Columbus came because Marco Polo
ventured Cathay. Behind their backs
we do not say the flower of democracy
blooms in China; we destine for that
celestial empire endless digging,
eradication of what's already loosely held,
write-downs and driveways.

Field Test

Weeds are a wild success—
escapees, some of them,
from cultivation.

They get up on the learning curve
faster than you can know their names
or trace their network.

But today I mowed into perfume
a whole patch of pineapple weed,
and not by mistake.

It made a sweeter task
of raising beds
to plant the pepper starts.

Their roots had never been plugged
and hung bare,
dripping an odorless new hormone.

Designed and synthesized
to keep the stress of transplant
from Georgia to New Jersey low,

to keep the stomata opening slow,
it so times the life that, when it swells,
each start should end in bells.

Tendrils

for Dick Wasson

They looked like twists of wire
on the wire line, the tendrils
of last year's grapevine,
but without the power to fasten.
Tight as mousetrap springs,
but their tension was gone.
They stayed without clinging.

The tractor mower blew them
round and round the wire.
Its blades took mouthfuls like a horse,
chewing salt hay with the vine,
spit it under blueberry bushes
the next row over.
The blueberries themselves hung tight.

Meanly at first I tore away
two thick vines like rebellion
in my way. Then I paused,
let the horsepower idle.
Obtrusive other vines ahead
I took like rope and set up
on the wire again,

the way my boss told me to,
tendril by tendril.
The new twists gripped
like caterpillars, but a wave
ran through them from the vines
wanting down. Resilience
can be a painful trait.

When I got going again,
another stem sprang down
with all its tendrils showing.
But I was by then as engaged
as the blades in my mowing.

On a Bus in Torino

He calls the *meridionali* shitheads,
says if he were still a soldier
he'd take them, break them up.

Spit's in his whiskers,
his umbrella's poised. "God fuck!
Pricks! You're wrong, you're wrong."

They've wrecked the ticket machine.
The soldier says how much it cost.
They cock their wrists.

The driver brakes.
"You know what you've done?
I did World War Two,

mother Mary fuck God.
I fought for you."
"Look, shit," one of them says,

"Get off here. Get the fuck off here."
A nun steps up between them.
Shithead says to shithead,

"Finish it. Finish it."
The nun says, "Enough."
"I know, sister," the soldier says,

"But mother Mary fuck God!
I did World War Two for them
and they bust the ticket machine."

"I know," says the sister.
The soldier stabs the floor,
shithead calls him a shit.

"There weren't kids like you
when I was a kid.
I did World War Two." Then he turns

to me. "Nice place for a foreigner,
Italy, isn't it?
I did World War Two. God's a pig."

Initiation by Aphasia

The camera and the woman
slip underwater at the same time.
She's naked, she carries a knife.

The star floats on his back,
laughing, smoking a cigar.
He doesn't know he's in for it.

Meanwhile, my little brother too
is happy. Training-wheels off,
he's balanced, coasting,

abandoned to the line
that will take him
safely through the turn.

The car he never saw was doing sixty.
I was getting a hard-on at the movie.
Not a word in either scene.

It's enough to make you never want to speak.
But my will was broken in a week,
and the pang has come to this.

III

By touch I perceive hard and soft, heat and cold, motion and resistance, and of all these more or less either as to quantity or degree.

—Bishop Berkeley, *Principles of Human Knowledge*, 1710

Touch

Close up, much too, ivory's surface like most
is nothing smooth. To the touch
in all particulars it's what the fresh
strawberry is to the tongue, cilia
bending at the buds after lunch. Specialists
in friction will tell you what pianists

with all of Mozart's sonatas in their heads
and hands will—except the ones who never
notice—that plastic slips and ivory catches,
the catch being what you want. To the touch:
everything is what it is to the touch,
algebra included, according to experts.

Skeptics to the contrary (unregistered
voters with unlisted numbers), we grant
the other hand as soon as we see the one.
Ivory will absorb what resin can't,
the heat of playing, the hands as they travel,
heightened, across the notes, beyond the scales

they're balanced in. Streets of asphalt, crashed on,
will scrape from the leg a subtle register
and make a subtler, sometimes called a strawberry.
You've seen one: the injured party
never lets you touch it. The days pass, though,
and the injured with a thumb discovers

a fresh surface beneath the scab—
just a sheen on the pink limit
between what the world calls skin, and flesh.

The New Century

Vienna revolts outside; in,
an addict is bent
over everything ever written on dreams
and hating it—but it has to be done,
to write the book, and he has to feel
a little unwell to write well.
Janus, his grubby old god
with the two faces—
no example extant,
Roman or Gothic,
possesses a third—
weights his writing down
while his hand,
under auspices that conflict,
riddles into plots
where Schliemann
had just been digging,
or so he thought,
deep as Mycenae and Troy.

Freud takes care, in his spare time,
what little he has, after walks
with his family in the park,
to avoid thinking. But the thing
that keeps taking his time
and making him think
is not that all the dreams
he's reading annoy him
with their dreamers'
insufferable cleverness,
or that he himself,
an insufferably clever
but shabby old Jew,

jokes of going to Rome
at Easter,
but that the new century,
whatever else it manifest,
is latent with his death—

which is intriguing;
but he's worked a little too
tremendously to bring forth
what, like most revelations,
is not so interesting
as the possibilities
discarded along the way—
to which, somewhat shaken,
he now returns.

Freudian Tenderness

Freud liked to collapse distinctions:
masochism is the continuation
of sadism ("nothing but"), in which
one's own person takes the place

of the sexual object; so looking
is analogous to touching; is based
on touching, is base in so far forth;
but neither the lingering at the touching

nor the lingering at the looking
satisfies the libido, the lust;
not the hunger, not the seeking,
not the loss, not the original

impulse or itch; here, there is no
base to touch, however corporate
the large series of factors may be
(conscience, castration complex),

however hard it is to believe
that a man who doesn't recognize you
two hours after meeting you
will recognize himself forty-three

years ago, tugging at his mother,
a charming woman with no clothes on.
There are all kinds of ways
to get into, and stay in, touch,

and the best excuse for not touching
is owning a person—which isn't
as easy as you might think. Many
are trying hard to come up with

original names, to achieve granularity,
to become dedicated paths on which
no noise conserves or returns
whatever is infantile and hurts.

Tenderness becomes hostility
("We are all somewhat hysterical")—
licking of feces, violation of cadavers,
the anatomical transgression itself

(body piercing body, cloning)—
highest and lowest everywhere
hanging together intimately
(no danger, here, of hanging separately);

shame, loathing, pain, fear;
anything bundling on or near
mouth, cell wall, anus:
but we cannot touch the fact.

The Difference

for Ruth Murphy Sweet

They had done such nice things.
He lay there as if he were almost
sleeping, don't you know.

My aunt took my hand
between hers. "No!"
I said, "I can't do that."

"Yes you can," she said.
Then she put my hand
on his cold hand

and pressed down.
Then she took my hand
away from my father's

and walked me away
from the coffin,
warming my hand in hers.

But I tell you, it made all the difference.

The Tactile Dome

the Exploratorium, San Francisco

Inside, we're told, "There's
nothing sticky or sharp,
but you won't be able
to see your hand
in front of your face,
which is kind of weird."
Weirder, I still wanted
to crouch or kneel or crawl,
to protect my head
(as if my hands
could never be put out.)

The exit was best,
a chute that dropped us
into a hill of beans,
our limbs in legume hands,
their skins between our toes.
The pleasure was sheer;
Pythagoras, wherever he is, knows.
Lima, pinto, kidney, string—
I wanted in without my clothes!

But children were there.
In that hemisphere of tact,
afraid to be blind and slow,
they tried to touch nothing
as fast as they could go
so that they could go again.
"That wasn't very hard,"
said one little boy,
who might have been Emerson:

Nothing can befall me in life,—
no disgrace, no calamity,
(leaving me my eyes,)
which nature cannot repair.

Concord Palinode

for Jon Adolph

Ragbags, imps of either, we lay prone
to find the thing to say. The snow there
chipped away at the snows of yesteryear,

as if it would cancel their accounts.
But the golf course grew only more pronounced,
and showed us where to take our fun.

What did we come up with that day, in a word?
What did we carry back with us from the run?
What from Concord backed us on the road home?

The Magyarest cabernet we ever tasted;
breakfast meats and beans; a definition
from the dictionary of Ambrose Bierce;

troubled thoughts about freedom wasted,
other people's, more than our own,
theirs seeming somehow twice as fierce.

What else? Nothing but this bounty?
The words that make us obnoxious:
"fictions," "repertory," "trope."

We're going to make a list like this
for a new edition of Aulus Gellius,
his Attic nights and etymologies,

when "late" began to mean "recent,"
and "reduce" (but I should check my notes)
had nothing to do with size.

Hitchcock, for instance, used the icicle;
Frost, a hot stove, a piece of ice;
Picasso, two parts of a bicycle.

What shall we use? It's all downhill from here.
Let's make dyslexia our device:
I'll work the pedals, you steer.

Lips

What new phylum rotates on my lips,
holds their place on the smoked trout
where I bit off more than I could chew?
No bigger than this (.) it stunned
the students of a lobster's lips.

I look hard at the lips of actors:
most are crooked, or thin, or overblown;
overbiting and lisping, underbiting, cleft;
but the camera likes them,
their owners exhibit them,

and I turn them over in my mind
for thickness, thinness, slant, lift,
pairing them with lips I've known,
tongued, bitten softly, sucked, kissed:
they all belong to Paula Bley.

That one mouth, repeating itself,
a small mouth, like a bass's, crooked
to the left and leaning, teeth never far
from showing, the two front and not
quite center setting each other in relief,

advanced and recessive; sweet tongue,
strong and good at kissing after school;
fetching, always clean: those lips were
surer of every word than Paula—now
Kirstie, now Meryl—through them ever

gave them credit for being. We would be
all mouth, if our heart were in the right
place, cuttlefish without ink, glomming on;
if only because, as the amateur electrician
put it, "everyone has to touch the ground

in common." Perhaps more phyla,
ready for their close-ups now,
await their students' thumbs-up
on the one mouth common to us,
whose lips are never sealed.

Architects

for Charles Sink

Architects are artichokes.
They have the hearts of them,
sheathe themselves in skin
like triceratops, stegosaurus.
They make an urban Dakota
hogback range run vertical,
razor and erector.

What is it in the afternoon
to vault up and peel
Magritte light, leaf by leaf,
from the room of the room?

The talking avenues,
the gridded streets,
fibrous, rigid, built to scale,
hold like a gum-pink resin.

Conic sections on a butter plate
stack up in the cowlick
of Philip Johnson's furniture—
those thin purple petals,
that rough hair like upholstery filling.

Then the perfect set of pores
that surface the concave lens: sweet place
where the stalk was crowned,
earth's weight attached.

Branches

for Catherine

You were out asking the night sky
who I live with and how you're supposed to be.

No wonder you can't study:
it's midnight, with its autointoxication,

and all the eucalyptus ramify
the "porcupine impossibility of contact"

between any one of you and any one of me.
Nothing is easy.

It's the distance we reach across
that we end up reaching;

it's the summer coming on,
your place by the ocean,

rough Pacifica's paradise,
beaches like the monkey tree's trunk,

lopped and lopped, knots holding
what were branches once

umbilical. But there are branches
still, as there are aims to dart to,

gulfs to shoot—fixed who knows
when or how—and paths, patches

of grass, endogenous palms like you.
Results are mixed, separations abrupt

("Tell me," you said, "one that isn't").

Blood Test

When the light gets in my smoke I fire;
I run through statement, over- to under-,
am tame to hold though I seem wild.

I would grab the smoke, not by where it
spreads into fingers in the glow,
but around its wrist at the navicular:

there's pulse and vanity so textbook
the phlebotomist paused twice before he dove.
Then fearsome red the blue blood ran.

It feels so good when I take you
"not by the hand, but round the arm
just above the wrist with a very firm,

strong hold," the way Emerson
took his oldest daughter,
guiding her "through a crowd

or across a brook.
It always felt very good."
I squeeze you tight there

when we walk—I talk as if we're walking—
but the ban is on, the break,
the smoke is in our eyes.

True love, true love!
Are we both Caesar's now,
that we touch each other not?

IV

. . . whoever is most intellectually motivated, most expert,
will seek to "touch" through his imagination and ideas . . . .
Nevertheless I feel sympathetic with anyone who does touch . . .

—Bernard Berenson, 1937

The Last Twenty Pages

It was too sweet for her this morning
when she walked with nothing in her hands,
hoping for feathers.

Later, she ran across the water
and tripped. You could tell
by her knees.

Now she lies in black
reading *Wide Sargasso Sea*,
the last twenty pages.

It's always the last twenty pages.
And no fishes when I swim into
warm places like napkin rings.

Both of us missed the light yesterday
that came clear under today
in almost unanimous shafts

the water grated. Above us
was tacking, floating, skiing,
mountain, sky.

Some were on land,
packing to leave and down about it,
and one was staying, a little girl,

to catch another frog and see it.
But none of us could be at home
on the water, or in it.

So most of the time we spent
was shored up for longing
after we went.

The Midnight Oil, an Ode to Psyche

I wish she comes to see me, my head up here
behind the window through the branches,
going back on all my words. But I take
precautions against her coming in,
up the loud stairs this late, to lay
claim, press in, make the many demands
I've invited. I turn no one away—
an infinitely appealing gesture,
complete with a safety
against the damage I've already done.
I don't have that much attention;
or no claim on it by any single guest
is reasonable: that's the situation
I create. Fortunately, things go wrong.

But how did she come by the notion
that my reaching out invited her grasp?
I must have set up hour after hour
in which I'd be available, I'd charm,
I'd flirt—perhaps as someone hampered
himself by loss, by need of care, by hurt.
If I would give her mine, she would give me hers,
as when I'd climb into the babysitter's lap,
winning her warmth, her hand on my head.
But love's the drawback of the sympathy
I drew on, whose name I'm afraid to speak.

Yet I've rarely been so completely unafraid.
I am the author of my being indisposed
to gratify the stars that run away,
the shadows that have eaten the moon.
A show of control is in itself enjoyable,
though someone in the room get stung.

When I told the man in the used-book store
that I was interested in everything,
he said: "Then you're interested in nothing,"
and turned away. He saw what he could see.

And I might have known that his help,
like what I wanted to be—unfaithful,
haphazard, helpless with impunity—
was out of the question. If she comes, then,
let her come as a threat to me,
bring her torch, burn my study down.

Cherry, Birch, Ash

for Brenda

The days will pass and we will forget them.
But yesterday, maybe never yesterday. I couldn't
even rake rocks in shade until I could tell you
I was gone out of my chest. I broke my toe-clip
riding to tell you, rode over the flattened glove
of another worker's hand heating up on the road,
right over the life-line's palm to downtown—
like a businessman. We met and leaned and thought
where to go. Vodka at the Wazee, an hour before
happy hour, two by two we drank until we thought it
strange we were not getting drunk. Then, at six,
a professor walks in who believes adultery
condemned in *The Scarlet Letter.*

I will find myself in your neighborhood again,
with something improvised to give you.
Ten miles away I have a feeling for your person,
what bar if you're not at home it might
do me some good to look in. Somehow,
you're in the alphabetical streets of trees,
Ash, Birch, Cherry—and now I know why:
it was Fantasy's where I watched you
being come up to, and that's on Detroit,
which is like no tree. You're an actress,
and you told me about the vapor-gapers,
Motown's forest of background vocalists.
Did you know me before, somehow? I was an actor,
and with a friend I'd down quarts of rum
in no time after shows, and when no shows ran;
would eat sugar-cubes whose centers slumped
with a drop of acid. And we wrecked a car!

Rum is on the brain now, lover—I see your
Lucy-headband, you breathe in, you breathe out:
the burden is easy, the burden is light.

My May and my West, my double and my trouble,
I want to bring out of you with my hands
your sadness, your pogo-stick brain
whose blunt end I am in the car—
your head on my lap, my hands on the wheel
most of the time, except now and then they
shade back your hair to let in on your face
the lamps of the avenue.

First Day of Spring

If the streetcars hadn't bunched up in the tunnel;
    if, an hour before that, I'd gotten out on time;
if I hadn't, like you, been late,
    I wouldn't have seen you being playful
at the bus-stop, walking the cement curb
    like a tightrope.
I wanted to ask if you were making up the rules
    as you went back and forth,
or were playing without them altogether,
    and so could never fault or win, be crowned or stripped.

And then you scrunched your hair—
    at which point I thought you looked a little tired,
but also fresh, refreshed, ready for whatever it was
    you were off to do next.
Lovely face, pretty eyes—no trace of fear
    in your bearing;
possessed of an animal happiness
    (Airedale? quarter horse? ocelot?),
you moved in the cage of our waiting there.

Then these things, on the bus:
    you work with flowers for money;
you box, you make art;
    you want to teach art in college;
you worry about a woman's cough
    (her lack of health annoys you);
you tell me you're a hooker
    (you make sure I know you're joking);
you light up and look me in the eyes when I tell you
    I teach; you think I don't
look old enough to be a professor,
    but you notice that I ask a lot of questions

(I have no time to explain);
 I tell you you remind me of Rebecca,
but I don't tell you all—how fearless, open, forward
 she was; how fresh, original, how much her own; and how,
for a summer and a fall, we were in love;
 I say instead, she's a photographer and an artist,
and I don't think she ever wanted to teach.

But we're looking for our streets now,
 wondering if we've missed them;
you say you're late, always late;
 you watch the coughing woman get off;
I see my street; you say,
 "Nice talking with you";
"Yes," I say, "nice talking with you";
 and get off to go hear Billy Joe Shaver
sing "Honky Tonk Heroes" and "Black Rose."

I turn to look once more to look at you,
 but you are turned the other way,
looking for California.
 I wish I knew your name (I feel a pang);
I wish you were coming along
 to the Great American Music Hall,
and we could talk some more about boxing and photography,
 flowers and teaching,
New York and California; your age and my age;
 lateness itself,
the earliest of things, the market for flowers;
 keeping one's hair the way one wants it;
the lines on sidewalks, the way shoes should hug feet;
 what being mellow amounts to;
why you showed me from your bag

what you wrap your hands in—your hands,
hands in general—but not what was in
    your other bag (lettuce, vegetables,
edible flowers?)—how the day at evening can sometimes
    begin again;
what a solid citizen you are, how soft the San Francisco air is.

Thompson Creek Road

for Stephanie

Why aren't those blue birds bluebirds?
This would be a meadow elsewhere,
but it doesn't seem called by the right name
when we call it meadow. What things are called,
how we speak of them: the German shepherd
holds the stick in his mouth like a cigar;
he punches other dogs with his paws.
The bear that clawed that aspen's long gone,
like a turkey through the corn. Some things
only language can see. We're not afraid of formulas:
the deep blue sky in Nepal—just like the deep blue
above us here, at the top of this ridge you thought
might look down over Sunlight. A false summit,
but a good place to rest and commemorate:
"That was good." And to go back down from,
drinking water from a jar that doesn't leak,
walking unawares, talking about pain.
(What awkward contact we can make.)
I've had my reasons not to go on; you say,
"Everyone does." But here I am, going on,
and getting along with you, right here,
farther up the creek than you've ever gone before.
It doesn't matter what the name of this place is:
it's original with us for now, and good enough
to be happy in, on balance, however used
the words we use, however green the new blue spruce,
and ungroomed the well-groomed trail we take.

Dilation

for Stephanie

When the moon, sun-like after dinner, decks itself out
for fun, and the stars, embarrassed, lie low,
I kiss the precious stones along your ear and lie,
against my wish, on my stomach. You see clouds,
clouds I wanted us to see together, larger in your eyes,
themselves dilated, taking measure, immense measure—
and Neil Diamond sings somewhere, "thank the Lord
for the night time, thank the Lord for you."

There are things larger than ourselves to feel sorry for,
to take pleasure in: this kiss, for one, and this, and this
still less tentative kiss, thirteen years in dilation.
And the cheek, the chin, the knee, the neck, the hair:
we're the same stuff, this non-attaching, unattached
liking-to-be-touched, and bound to suffer for our fun,
and be grateful; to move, fearing death, and to keep
moving under whatever sky night and day give us.

So your face, in the moonlight spreading, in the laughter
of light sleep and deep depression, in the sweet
cave where your hair comes down, my forehead
on your chest, so obvious; and then the meadowlark,
confused perhaps by the range of the moon's almost
summer day, sings beyond the ticking of my watch,
its face big as your pupil, occluding all but iris-edge:
and we look, and we see, and we will see.

Dawn Finished

Deep road back in the woods,
the high one on Mount Sanitas,
full moon, midnight to the dawn-side,
timberline nearer, the single cabin
warm and lit, like a candle's conductor
or an orchestra's pit. *I love everything*

by turns and nothing long, survive
the usefulness of every feeling
or two days, whichever comes first;
blame not the slain father, like a damper
on the wires, but the living one;
not the dead God or the mother denied,

who was so good at that herself, so
stealthily betrayed; but she who was
always there alone with you alone—
dawn finished but not yet day,
the sprinklers dripping, the woodchips
refusing flame, the romance too dark

for the workshop—all tender things—
fresh asphalt, white clouds, rain
surfacing a court, the net taut.
Then again the blue, together with this
t–shirt shade of green,
the blue that is the deepest.

A Friend

You said you knew you were loved
in your family, but it was always
like an air conditioner on low,
cool, and you had no power.
I told a friend what you said,
then asked him, was he loved in his?
He said his mother loved no one
and his father was the most forgiving man.

It made for combustion, he said,
but they could do nothing with it.
Then there are people with framework
and some principle of pleasure,
people who know about broken hearts
outside of books. They have no place
to refer you; they tell you
to get out of your head—

which is what your mother,
the intuitive one, like you,
has always said. But where would you go?
You didn't know where to go,
outside of lying, outside of
seeing no point in the morning
to the day, to the migraine,
to the appetiteless eating and fucking

and the fretting that burned out
wherever it was you lived.
So you didn't like stories,
but you read them. In poetry,
you sought the elliptical,
the English, the Larkin,
and couldn't care in song
for any but the sad cabaret.

Where had your life gone,
that you lived it so long this way?
There was always kindness and beauty
and truth, but they weren't enough.
You thought there was love,
but that wasn't enough, not the ballgame.
And so you're open now,
if your mother doesn't ask you

what your dreams are,
if the apartment comes through
you can have your bath in.
You know what it is to be wanted now,
to have a friend, to be the one
another wants to spend time with.
You have heard—
You come too, you come too.

The Scott Boys

Slapped by saplings, hampered by roots,
our shovels went like spoons
into mouth that opened wider as we worked.
The fort when we finished
was as cool to go down in
as a thimble for a fingertip.

But even when we dug all day,
we could still make out
from where we leveled off
the greenish-gray of house
above the cheatgrass
doubling over in the sun.

The mountains must've been
too far to reach by hand,
the elms not branched enough to climb.
We never knew we were doing anything
but digging a deeper hole
than the one we dug before.

Buildings went up;
we were building down,
like the Grand Canyon,
from an overrated sky;
and we hoped we'd see by digging
if maybe we couldn't find

a better place to be than upstairs—
solider, smaller, a back-up
we could back down in.

The Cave of AIDS

in memory of Craig William Scott (1961–1984)

> It annoys him to speak,
> and it hurts him not to.
> —W. H. Auden, "The Cave of Nakedness"

It was when you were dying
and you couldn't speak
that we loved you the most.

Mom and Dad were still doing
the wrong things the best they knew how.
Again you couldn't use the kind of

attention that they gave;
but all of us were out to annoy you,
because it hurt that you didn't speak.

Maybe there were forty words from you
in what was to be the last week
you breathed, sipping at the surface

like a trout when it feeds.
Drop by drop, the morphine
let us all go on. Into your arm

it went, and it held our tongues.
It got beyond what was healthy,
your keeping to yourself,

our ancient live-and-let-live,
each of us safekeeping. Your privacy's
blank as your diary now.

What annoyed and hurt you,
you held until you couldn't eat,
you couldn't walk, you couldn't speak.

So we started talking. We left you
the room to die in, and went into the hall.
We said: he will die when he is ready.

And I think you did.
You yellowed and smelled
like the salamanders

we'd catch in the skimmers
before we'd swim,
and then you went in.

Accumulations

One cigarette before bed
a couple has learned to smoke,
one each, in bed, before they sleep
and dream dreams that sunder them, oh,
thousands of miles, thousands of times.
It takes an abundance of hunger
to be able to do that, it must,
when the smoking lamps go out
without the aid of war.
You have read the book that closes
on bitter ash just once too often,
because it hasn't made sense again .
and again. Ash is supposed to be
the cleanest substance known to us,
and how can what is clean be bitter?
Because there was that experiment
the biology class did in high school:
the hands, the more you wash them,
the more interesting the culture
their lines produce in the petri dish.
And then at home, in a happy hour,
some patriarch, avidly mixing, discovered
that bitters makes the old-fashioned better.
For over a year now, the days have passed
without giving rise to that hour,
sugarless days, light evenings, dry nights.
Evidence mounted, favoring the bent of addicts,
like ice in the kitchen freezer,
until the arm that started the process
couldn't lift away the made ice
to make more. Everything is cubed.
The old lead green-eyed cat
that used to stop my grandmother's door

sits on the windowsill stopping dust,
and stares at fulfillment
between what's-his-name and the ceiling.
I am trying to believe in all
the test results I can, but a run
of accumulating negatives must end
in disaster, like those referenda
whose phrasing makes you think
more than twice before you say, I do.
Clean bills of health are getting
harder and harder not just to come by,
but to pay, and believe in.
Since something is wrong with us,
what's another accident, or a couple
packs of cigarettes, while we wait
in the meantime for the next results.

Fruit Country

Certain fruits, like bananas and crabapples,
record everything that happens to them,
and this is called "getting ripe."
But I am too late or too soon,
and this banana I take a knife to
when I can't talk in time
takes in what I give off
and gives it out again.

Experts say bananas are best eaten
black, when their starch converts
to sugar, and we throw them out.
At Fruit Country, only a retired pilot
asked us to save him black bananas.
He seemed always on the point
of bleeding dry through his pores.
His watch slid down to his elbow
when he'd hold a bunch up to the light.

A picture of perfect health is rare,
in spite of all the scenarios there are
for developing one, the clubs and spas
that promise the body of an excellent
white wine, a buttery nose, a clean finish.
But who's to say this brown and spreading blotch
I pressure the crabapple into making,
this nick's assimilation in the pear,
isn't a blow struck for beauty?

The peach sweetens in its bruises.
Ripeness owns its uses.

When I Die

Shall I tell you what to say?
I think about it all the time.
Do this first: look at all the notes I made.
And the sheets of calendars I saved.
You won't find certain things,
so don't worry about covering me.
I knew a baseball from a cycling cap.
I knew what was going on
on my side of the table.
Say I lied where my feelings were concerned—
without compunction say it.
When it comes to friends, hesitate,
but notice that I had too many,
and none but my father depended on me.
Him I didn't let down, not even now:
even today's accomplishment he envies.
Say that for a model I used my mother:
those whose hearts I broke were always
welcome around me in the kitchen.
In the notes you'll find very little
to go on, since I never took down
the depths. I doubted their existence
beyond my sixteenth year. That I never
set out to hurt anyone is a lie
that bears repeating nonetheless.
But to tell the truth that I was not
different—this will get you (and who
shall you be?) borne away on the wings
of disbelief. Add that I loved myself.
Add that near the end. Tack it on
just before you close, not because I did,

but because it will kill my father.
He is, I know, afraid of dying,
but he wants to be immortal.
Our secret lay in not dying daily,
but in wishing to, and telling no one.

Viewers Like You

Viewers like you have seen stills
of birds humming at nectar,
their maintenance a blur;
or time-lapse footage
of birds building nests,
their autism cut by an editor.

But to say *Hamlet* was composed
as a bird builds a nest
is not to say the play's organic.
Take a pair of house finches:
they perched; they darted; they lit again
and screamed, pecking and pacing
the aluminum window frame.
And then they forgot about it,
their own succession.

A strand of what looked like vinca
was all they brought up in that hour—
maybe one line. And nothing there
to add it to or put it in, except
what a patient's need for fresh air
afforded them, a tight slot
along the frame. Another pair
might've chosen the ledge.

On the other side of the clinic,
in the same situation,
another pair completed a nest.
In a month, I never saw them
building, never saw them light.
But a niche of shreds and patches,
dilations that I missed,
grew there like a stage for those antic birds
that had no arras, no daggers, no words.

photo by Elizabeth Ruth Scott

Mark Scott was born in Denver, and studied at the University of Colorado, University College London, and the Università per Stranieri in Perugia. He took his doctorate in literature at Rutgers, the State University of New Jersey, in 1992. His poems have appeared in *Raritan*, *The Paris Review*, *The Kenyon Review*, *Poetry*, and other journals. He has taught literature at Mills College, San Francisco State, and the University of San Francisco. He lives in Colorado.

New Issues Poetry & Prose

Editor, Herbert Scott

James Armstrong, *Monument in a Summer Hat*
Anthony Butts, *Fifth Season*
Gladys Cardiff, *A Bare Unpainted Table*
Lisa Fishman, *The Deep Heart's Core Is a Suitcase*
Joseph Featherstone, *Brace's Cove*
Robert Grunst, *The Smallest Bird in North America*
Edward Haworth Hoeppner, *Rain Through High Windows*
Josie Kearns, *New Numbers*
Lance Larsen, *Erasable Walls*
David Dodd Lee, *Downsides of Fish Culture*
Deanne Lundin, *The Ginseng Hunter's Notebook*
Joy Manesiotis, *They Sing to Her Bones*
David Marlatt, *A Hog Slaughtering Woman*
Paula McLain, *Less of Her*
Malena Mörling, *Ocean Avenue*
Julie Moulds, *The Woman With a Cubed Head*
Marsha de la O, *Black Hope*
C. Mikal Oness, *Water Becomes Bone*
Margaret Rabb, *Granite Dives*
Rebecca Reynolds, *Daughter of the Hangnail*
Martha Rhodes, *Perfect Disappearance*
John Rybicki, *Traveling at High Speeds*
Mark Scott, *Tactile Values*
Diane Seuss-Brakeman, *It Blows You Hollow*
Marc Sheehan, *Greatest Hits*
Phillip Sterling, *Mutual Shores*
Angela Sorby, *Distance Learning*
Russell Thorburn, *Approximate Desire*
Robert VanderMolen, *Breath*
Martin Walls, *Small Human Detail in Care of National Trust*
Patricia Jabbeh Wesley, *Before the Palm Could Bloom:
    Poems of Africa*